# DATE DUE

| | | | |
|---|---|---|---|
| NOV 18 '92 | | | |
| MAR 3 '93 | | | |
| APR 8 '93 | | | |
| OCT 1 '93 | | | |
| JAN 7 1994 | | | |
| MAR 9 1994 | | | |
| | | | |
| | | | |
| | | | |
| | | | |
| | | | |
| | | | |
| | | | |
| | | | |
| | | | |

# WHY DO PEOPLE DRINK ALCOHOL?

All photographs were taken with models and obtained from photographic agencies except those on pages 7, 18, 27 and 28.

© Aladdin Books 1989

*Designed and produced by*
Aladdin Books Ltd, 70 Old Compton Street, London W1V 5PA

Editor: Catherine Bradley
Design: Rob Hillier
Illustration: Ron Hayward Associates
Research: Cecilia Weston-Baker
Consultant: Angela Grunsell

Pete Sanders is the head teacher of a North London elementary school and is working with teachers on personal, social and health education.

Angela Grunsell is an advisory teacher specializing in development education and resources for the primary school age range.

*Published in the United States in 1989 by*
Gloucester Press, 387 Park Avenue South, New York, NY 10016

ISBN 0 531 17134 5

Library of Congress Catalog
Card Number: 88-83102

# "LET'S TALK ABOUT"

# WHY DO PEOPLE DRINK ALCOHOL?

## PETE SANDERS

**Gloucester Press**
New York · London · Toronto · Sydney

Some choose to drink alcohol, others choose to drink fruit juices.

# "What is alcohol?"

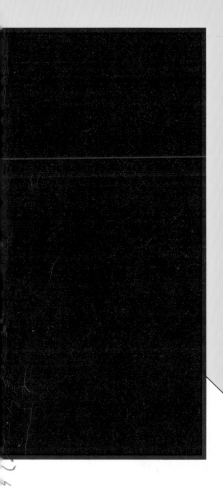

Think of all the drinks you have seen. They don't taste the same because they are made from different things. Some of them have alcohol in them.

Alcohol is a chemical. It is made by tiny living things called yeasts. There are many kinds, including drink and paraffin. Yeasts can be found on fruit skins and any sugary fruit will turn into alcohol if it is left for long enough. Alcohol is a legal drug – anyone of age can drink it. People have been drinking it for thousands of years.

Beer is made from hops, grains, barley and yeast. Grapes are used to make wine. Other drinks have grains in them which have been boiled. The steam that is produced cools and turns into a liquid, such as vodka, rum and whisky. These are called "spirits."

All alcoholic drinks have water in them. The amount of alcohol varies. In most beers about five percent is alcohol. Wines have about 12 percent alcohol but in spirits it's about 50 percent. The more alcohol there is, the more effect it will have on the drinker.

The main picture shows beer being brewed. The sugar from barley is mixed with yeast. When the mixture begins to bubble, it means alcohol is being made. (The background is wine.)

# "What happens to alcohol in the body?"

You may have heard someone say drinking alcohol "goes to my head." In fact it travels around the body. First it goes into the stomach and then the alcohol travels through the bloodstream. It is carried to the brain and affects the brain's control of the body. Alcohol can make people behave and feel completely different.

Drinking a lot of alcohol over a long period of time damages the body. Alcohol is a drug – it changes the way the body works.

## The brain
You may forget things and find it difficult to think clearly. The more alcohol you have, the more this will happen.

## The heart
Alcohol makes your heart beat faster. This means your blood travels around your body more quickly.

## The stomach
Drinking too much alcohol upsets the stomach and can lead to ulcers, irritations of the stomach.

## The liver
The liver gets rid of things in food we don't need. If people drink too much alcohol, the liver may stop working.

9

# "How does alcohol make you feel?"

Alcohol has a different effect on different people. It can make you feel happy or sad depending on your mood. When you've been upset, has anyone ever tried to cheer you up by giving you a treat? Sometimes it works, at other times it doesn't. However, if you drink too much it can make you feel very ill.

Have you ever felt giddy on a merry-go-round? Some people feel like that after drinking alcohol.

When people drink the way their body moves is affected. You can get clumsy after a few drinks. Alcohol can also change what people understand and how they work things out.

Alcohol can make you feel excited at first and then sleepy. It can even make you thirsty. It can alter the way people speak as well as what they say. It can affect your memory. And like any drug, it can help block out hurt. But it can also give you pain.

Too much alcohol causes a hangover, which includes a bad headache. You might even be sick. You can feel that you are out of control – unable to do things you could normally do.

People often arrange to meet friends in a place where alcoholic drinks are sold. Enjoying a drink can be fun but your friends may try to talk you into drinking when you don't want to.

# "Why do people drink alcohol?"

People drink alcohol for lots of reasons – not just because they are thirsty. Drinking is seen as a way of being friendly. After a few drinks you can feel less shy and awkward, but you can also make a fool of yourself.

Drinks are used at parties or to celebrate special occasions, like a birthday or holiday. Alcohol is also used in cooking food to make a special meal. Alcohol is used in some religious ceremonies – for example, wine in a Catholic mass.

Some people drink to look more grown up or because they think it will help them feel they belong in a group. Others say having a drink cheers them up.

Certain boys think that drinking alcohol makes them seem more like a man. Being able to drink a lot and not look drunk is important to some people. Girls might drink to show they can keep up with the boys. It may make them feel more relaxed so they do things they wouldn't normally do.

You may know people who don't drink alcohol at all. They may not like the taste or smell or they may have religious beliefs that don't allow them to drink. Some people don't like the effect alcohol has on them.

Some people drink a little beer or wine at family meals. They enjoy the way it makes them feel. If you choose to drink alcohol, you need to know how it affects you and how much you can drink. If you don't want to drink, saying no can be hard.

17

Driving after drinking alcohol is very dangerous. Half the drivers killed in crashes have had too much alcohol.

# "What's wrong with drinking alcohol?"

Have you ever started to do something you can't stop yourself from doing – like biting your nails? Some people get into the habit of drinking, and feel that they can't do without alcohol. This can cost a lot of money. Sometimes it stops them from doing important things like being with their families or being at work.

Alcohol can spoil the way people treat each other. It can lead to bad moods, fights and accidents. It can lead to an illness called alcoholism.

# "What is an alcoholic?"

An alcoholic is someone who can't stop drinking and who plans life around having a drink. Even though this causes problems, alcoholics continue drinking. This can make life very difficult for those who live or work with an alcoholic. An alcoholic may not even realize that drinking is a problem.

Some parents are alcoholics. Often their children have to make excuses for them. These children may feel very lonely, perhaps angry too. It's important for them to talk to someone about those feelings.

# "What kind of people become alcoholics?"

You may think that alcoholics are easy to spot. This is not true. There are many people who drink every day but not all of them are alcoholics. Anyone can become an alcoholic — from mothers and fathers to students and business people. Drinking is a way some people try to forget problems like boredom or stress. It is very difficult for an alcoholic to give up drinking.

Heavy drinking can make you feel less lonely for a while but it also creates problems.

24

# "How can you stop people from drinking too much?"

Many people think that warnings about the dangers of alcohol should be written on the labels of cans and bottles, like they are on cigarette packs, though these warnings do not stop smokers from smoking. But there are laws to stop people from driving if they drink more than a certain amount. Most countries do not allow young people to buy alcohol.

The police use breathalyzers to check if drivers have too much alcohol in their bodies.

Some countries, such as Saudi Arabia, don't allow people to buy alcohol at all. This doesn't stop people from drinking. In the United States in the 1930s drinking alcohol was illegal. Prohibition, as this was called, didn't work because people broke the law to get alcohol.

Another idea is to make alcoholic drinks very expensive. But many governments don't seem to want to do this because it might be unpopular. The companies who make and sell alcoholic drinks don't want people to stop drinking because they would make less money.

During Prohibition in the United States, supplies of alcohol were destroyed.

27

Advertisements try to make you think drinking is what smart people do. They make alcholic drinks look tempting.

# "Is alcohol a problem?"

Often it is easier to blame others when we don't want to own up to something which is our own fault. People blame alcohol for things they have done or said. Yet they find it hard to admit this. It's hard to face up to problems.

When you watch television, take a look at how people with drinks are shown. Do they look good? It's odd that drinking is shown as being normal. Yet for some it can be dangerous.

# "What can I do?"

Many people become drinkers because drinking is part of everyday life. It is important for us to know what happens when we drink alcohol. It is a powerful drug that can take over people's lives.

If you are worried about someone you know who has a drinking problem and need someone to talk to, you can contact the organizations listed below. For more information about alcohol education contact Alcoholics Anonymous.

**Addresses for more information**

Al-Anon Family Groups
P.O. Box 862
Midtown Station
New York, New York 10018

Women's Alcoholism Center
2261 Bryant Street
San Francisco, California 94110
(415) 282-8900

# What the words mean

**Alcohol:** A liquid made by fermenting sugar. It is in cider, beer, wine and spirits.

**Beer:** A drink made from yeast, barley and hops, which has a small amount of alcohol.

**Breathalyzer:** A bag you blow into, which gives a rough measure of how much alcohol is in your blood.

**Drug:** Anything you put in your body, other than food, that changes the way it works.

**Spirits:** A very strong alcoholic drink which can be half alcohol, half water.

**Wine:** A drink made from grapes, which usually has a small amount of alcohol.

# Index

**Photographic Credits:**
Cover: CVN Pictures; pages 4 and 7 (background): Robert Harding Library; page 7 and 18: Zefa; pages 8 and 11: Magnum; pages 13 and 23: Network; pages 14, 16 and 21: Richard and Sally Greenhill; page 24: Rex Features; page 27: Keystone; page 28: Nicholas Enterprises.